# SEO

CW00860203

## Learn Advanced Search Engine Optimization Marketing Secrets, For Optimal Growth! Best Beginners Guide About SEO For Keeping your Business Ahead in The Modern Age!

**Graham Fisher**

# Table of Contents

# Introduction

Times are changing and the internet is becoming the main way to add success to your business. Whether you write a blog or own a restaurant, you need your online profile to represent the greatness of your brand. You also need people to find your information from online searches. If you own a children's toy store, you want your results to come up not only when people search "the best toy store" but also when they search the best places to shop in your specific city. You especially want to make sure that your business shows up in the search results when people are searching specifically for you.

So, how can you make sure these things are happening? You need to learn all about SEO, or Search Engine Optimization. Search engine optimization makes sure that when people are searching online, they find your business right where you want them to. It ensures the searches that display the best sides of your company allow you to show up in the results. It can also ensure that you get to be at the very top of the page.

In this book, we are going to take you from not knowing much about search engine optimization to being a complete SEO expert. We are going to share what SEO is, how you can do it, and what results come from what actions. We will answer all of your big questions and we will explain things that you may not even yet know exist. We will give you the tips and the tricks you need to optimize your business's SEO to your very best ability.

If you are ready to become an SEO expert, you have come to the right place. We are excited to help you learn and we know that our book is the very best resource to learn all about search engine optimization.

# Chapter One: What is Search Engine Optimization?

The first thing we need to learn while we are looking into how to best represent your business in search results is what exactly search engine optimization is. To start with this topic, let's look into how Google works.

So to start, we all know that Google started its days as simply a search engine. This is the part of the Google company that we need to learn about, so as we refer to Google, we will be referring to its search engine capabilities.

Google works by using algorithms based on what you type into its search bar. It also uses things called spiders, or crawlers, to search for information all over the internet. The main thing that Google runs on, however, is something called Keywords. Keywords are the main base of search engine optimization and they are something that you will completely master creating by the end of this book. We will look into keywords in great detail in the next chapter, learning what they are, why they are important, and exactly how to use them to benefit you and your business as much as possible. For now, just remember that they are extremely important in the way that Google works.

Another thing that is important in how Google works is that it looks into how long websites have existed. If your website has been around for years, it has a much better probability of showing up in a Google search than a website that was just created yesterday. Google does this because websites are easy to create and surprisingly, new websites are actually created every single day from all around the world. Some of these websites become a big deal. Think of Facebook, for example. One day it was just a brand new website. A few years later, it was something that everyone in the world knew about and something that most people in more privileged countries use on a daily basis. Other websites, however, maybe like the nutrition blog your old high school classmate started on a whim, will be posted to three or four times and then forgotten about and/or given up on. Google needs to tell the difference between these two types of sites, which shows why it matters not only how good your site is, but also how long it has been around online.

Google also looks into how much traffic, or how many people are clicking on and visiting your online site, your webpage is getting. A website that has only been clicked on three hundred times is much less relevant to what a person is searching for than a website that has been vied many millions of times. When people search on Google, they are usually looking for accurate results and usable information. If a site has been clicked on many times, Google knows that the information it has is useful and relevant.

Lastly, Google also looks at how many other sites online have clickable links that direct viewers to the website. If your site is referred to by many other websites and there are many links out there that direct right to your site, Google knows that people online like your information. They know that people refer you as a great source, which allows them to believe that you are a great source as well. This is actually the best way to get your site to show up in Google searches because they put so much trust in your website when other real people continue to refer it and advertise it.

So far we know that Google works through keywords, the age of websites, how much traffic a website gets, and how many links direct to a website. These things all make sites show up higher in search results and without these things, results are obviously much lower. It is also important to note, however that Google keeps some secrets as to how it works as well. It is definitely the best search engine available and everyone who uses the internet knows this. If Google gave away all of their secrets and every piece of how their search engine worked, other search engine sites would be able to copy them. They would then no longer stand out as the top search engine, so of course they cannot share all of their information with us.

These are the most commonly used ways in which Google ranks websites for their search results, but let's look into the entire top ten ranking factors that they use as well. We can never have too much information on how Google works, because we want our website to fit exactly what they are looking for in order for it to show up as a top result.

1. The first ranking factor for Google is making sure that your website is safe and secure. It cannot have links to viruses or other malicious sites or software, because people trust google to only bring them to safe sites. Google needs to keep up this reputation by not listing sites that are not safe and secure. In this same category, your site also needs to be easy to access. If it is a website that people cannot see or people have a hard time seeing, this hurts Google's reputation as well. People want results that will help them, not things that they cannot see. Because of this, Google

will not rank your site high if it is not easily accessible.

2. The second thing that Google looks into is the speed of your website. People do not like to wait a long time for things to load. Because of this, your website needs to be quick in order to show up well in Google search results.

3. The third thing Google looks into is that your site is able to be viewed well on mobile devices. This is because almost all of the web surfing that happens today is happening on smartphones. People still use computers often, but the typical simple Google search is done on phones more often than not. If your website only loads well on a computer screen and is difficult to use from a smartphone, it will not rank high in Google search results.

4. The fourth thing that Google looks into is how long your website has been around on the internet, which we looked into previously.

5. The fifth thing that Google looks into on your site is how relevant and useful your information is. If your information does not match the searches, it obviously will not show up in the results. For example, if you have a pizza parlor your website will not show up

when someone searches for "dog groomer near me".

6. Google of course also looks into technical SEO. We will discuss this in great detail later, but it involves keywords, web analytics, and other technical features of the search engine results.

7. The experiences that users of Google have on your site is important as well. Google uses a site called RankBrain to see what people around the world think of different websites. The ones that are well-enjoyed will show up in the top search results while the ones with bad reviews or no reviews will not show up well.

8. As well mentioned earlier, links that lead to your website are extremely important as well. This detail has a heavy weight in Google's decision on where to rank your site.

9. Social signals are important to Google. This includes the amount of traffic, or visitors, that view your site as well mentioned earlier as well as how your site does on social media, which we will look into in great detail later in the book.

10. The last thing that Google looks into while they are ranking your site is that you have information about a real business. If your site

leads to a real place, it will show up much higher in search results. This tool is especially important to pay attention to when you are creating a site that you want people to find who are local and close to you, which we will also look into in great detail in another chapter of this book.

The reason why we need to know how Google works is because it helps us to ensure that our results rate well in every category that they look into. Now, let's look into some things that used to help in search engine optimization but are no longer useful at all.

The first thing that people used to do but should no longer do, is to add many links to your web content just to look better to Google. Google has changed to look at the quality of your links and not the quantity of them. If your site links to ten small sites that have little to no traffic, it will not show up in search results as well as a site that has two great, highly visited sites linked into their content.

This also means that if your twenty mom-blog friends link to your website, it may not help you very much in terms of your SEO. However, if you get a link to your site from a well-known company, this will help your SEO greatly.

The next thing that people used to focus on but should not anymore is making sure they always have the number one spot on Google. Google today is filled with ads, so even if you are the number one result, you may not show up at the top of the page. This also means that people are more likely to scroll down and pick the result they find the most helpful or interesting. Because of this, you are just as well off if you appear in the top five results rather than going out of your way and wasting time, energy, and resources to be the number one.

It is also important to remember that your main goal is to make a website that people like and that they can benefit from. It needs to represent your business well. If your site does not do this, it does not matter where you show up in search results. You may have high traffic, but people will leave your site quickly if it is not helpful or enjoyable.

Because of this, do not focus too much on SEO. If SEO is the only thing you focus on, you may forget the purpose of your website. If you forget your purpose, you will have a great SEO result and a website that no one likes.

People also used to make sure that their websites were huge with many pages and a large amount of information. If you do this, you may forget to make posts that are again useful and that people enjoy. This is an area where quality is much more important than quantity. A few useful posts and pages are much better and more appreciated that one hundred sites that do not have the information that people are looking for.

Also, you need to be careful with your keywords. Logically, more keyword usage will make your results show up higher in Google. However, if you use your keyword too often, it will be difficult for readers to understand your content. If you use your keyword incorrectly, it will definitely turn people away.

Overall, when you are building a website today you need to pay more attention to the people who will be visiting it than the SEO. Of course you still need to use SEO tools to help people find your site easily and quickly, but use them tastefully. This is a switch in mindset from how SEO used to be used. It is, however, a very important thing to understand.

Another thing to pay attention to when working on your SEO are the three pillars of SEO success. These include Authority, Trust, and Relevance. These three pillars mean exactly what you probably think they mean. Authority means that you need to ensure that your audience (and Google) believe that you are a person that they should listen to about the topic you are writing about. Do you own the business that the page is for? Do you have a doctorate degree in the subject being discussed? Do you have many years of experience in the business or topic being discussed?

If so, you have the authority to speak on that topic or business. For trust, you simply need to make sure that what you are writing can be trusted. Is your information from personal experience? Do you cite sources or include links to where you found the information? Is your writing honest and are your reviews truthful? If so, your readers (and Google) can trust you. Lastly, relevance makes sure that the topics you write about on your site go along with the information people are searching for. For example, if you have a food blog and people come to you for recipes, post about food and not articles about horses or something else completely unrelated. Following these three pillars of success will help you SEO and will keep readers happy with your website.

It is also extremely important to note when speaking of Google, that their algorithms change and their website updates. It is very important to stay ahead of these updates. If a big update takes place and things change drastically, your SEO could suffer. To avoid this, pay attention to the news on this topic. Follow along with reported upcoming updates and research them to see if they are real. If they are, be ready to change things up to optimize SEO in the latest way possible.

# Chapter Two: Keyword Research- The Most Important Step of SEO

As we mentioned at the very beginning of our book, keywords are the most important thing to know about and to use correctly when looking into your search engine optimization (SEO). In this chapter, we will look into keywords in detail. We will discuss what keywords are, why keyword research is so important, how to find keywords, how to use keywords, and more.

First, let's figure out what a keyword actually is. A keyword is a word that explains your article. It is a word that when someone types it into the Google search bar, you would like your article to be in one of the top spots in the result list. It is a word that when searched, your webpage would be an accurate result that would give searchers the exact information that they were looking to find.

Next, let's look into why keywords are important. Keywords are the sole way that Google decides what searches will lead to your page. The other factors that Google uses determines your ranking within the results, but your keywords are the reason why you are found in that specific list at all. Without keywords, you would not turn up in the right search results. You would not be found where you want your readers to find you. Google would not know if your content was relevant to your main subjects.

Overall, keywords are your way to have control over where you show up in search engine results. They allow you to appear in certain searches and not in others, and they put the control of this in your own hands. If you do not take action over this control, your SEO will suffer greatly.

So, let's look into how you can use this tool to your fullest ability. First of all, you need to do research on your keywords. Researching your keywords allows you to see what other results come up with the keywords that you are thinking of using. You can do this type of keyword research by simply typing in your word or phrase into the Google search bar and looking at the list of results.

You can do another type of keyword research as well. You can use certain websites and type in your keyword, and they will help you to know which keyword will generate the most traffic to your site. One site like this is moz.com.

Another way to tell if a keyword is good or not is to buy a sample campaign from a site like Google AdWords. This would basically be buying an advertisement that would show up based on the keyword that you chose. You could make the traffic that came from clicking the ad redirect to your website. By doing this, you would be able to tell how much traffic was generated by the keyword and if it was useful or not.

Next, let's look into how you can find and choose keywords. First, a good way to find keywords is to use an online tool that will help you to generate a massive list of them. One of these tools is again within GoogleAdWords. In this program, there is a keyword tool. This tool will make a huge list of keywords for you. It will also tell you how much traffic is typically generated from each keyword. Keywordtool.io is another option for keyword research. This site is nice because when you type in your keyword, it allows you to click on different sites like YouTube and Amazon to see how well your keyword would work. This makes the tool usable not only for Google results but videos and selling products as well.

These tools can not only be used to find keywords that will work for you, but also to ensure that the keywords you choose will make traffic come to your site. As we mentioned earlier, they can tell you which keywords bring traffic to your site and approximately how much traffic they can bring as well.

We mentioned earlier in the book that Google ranks your content based on how relevant it is to its searches, but how does it do this? How does Google know what you website is even about? Let's look into these questions and figure out how we can optimize our SEO in this way.

The way that Google knows what your web page is about is through On Page SEO. On Page SEO is search engine optimization techniques that show on your website, not external links. External links help to your Google result rankings, but On Page SEO tells Google what you are talking about.

Let's now look into the different types of On Page SEO. The first and most important component in On Page SEO is the content of your site. It's what the person searching is actually looking for, so it is what Google puts the biggest emphasis on.

Next, On Page SEO needs a title tag. A title tag is something that shows up in the web address and it is also what will show up on Google as the title of the website. You need a good title tag so that Google can rank you higher and so that people can see an interesting title to click on when they see your search engine result.

The next thing that a good On Page SEO needs is an acceptable URL. The URL should tell the reader what the website is going to talk about. If it simply has a chain of random letters and numbers, it will not rank as high on Google and will not be as well understood by your site visitors.

Now that we have looked at On Page SEO, let's look into how you can structure your web page for easy and automatic SEO. We all know that running a business or a webpage can be hard work. If anything can be done automatically for you or at least easily by you, it can be a big help.

Before we look into how to structure your site, though, let's look into why this is so important. The first reason why the structure of your site is important is because it makes a good experience for the people who visit your site. This is important because the more people that are happy with your site, the more people will visit it and possibly even help you out by linking to your pages.

Also, if your structure is set up right, your Google search result will have site links listed. This is when your main page is listed as a Google result, but in smaller form underneath this result are links to your other pages. This not only makes your Google result look more professional, but helps visitors to get to the place they want or need easily as well, which in turn optimizes user experience again.

Remember how we talked a little bit about how Google uses spiders, or crawlers, in the beginning of our book? Well, if your site has a good structure, these spiders of crawlers are able to navigate your web page better and find more information, which allows you to rank higher in Google results without much effort on your part.

Now that we know why site structure is so important, let's learn what you really want to know. How can you structure your site for optimal SEO? First, you will want to make a type of hierarchy with your site information. This means that you will start with your main page, and that main page will have a few segments to other pages of your site. These other pages with have links to a few of your other pages which will have links to a few other pages and so on. It is almost like building a pyramid. You start with the broadest and most important information and let things trickle down the line. The most important thing to remember when you are building your pyramid is to make sure that your order makes sense. Then, make sure that your number of pages or articles is not overwhelming. Consider keeping more than two but less than seven links to main categories from your home page. Lastly. Make sure that the number of subcategories that each category has is an equal or somewhat equal number. For example, do not have one category have two subcategories and the other category have ten subcategories.

Another thing to pay attention to when building the structure of your website is the structure of your URL. Just as it is important that your URL is readable and makes sense, it is also important that your URL follows the structure that your web page follows. This will help Google to understand the structure of your site and it will make for a better user experience at the same time.

Something called a shallow depth structure in regards to navigation is important as well. This means that to access the information on your site, visitors should need to click only one, two, or three times. If they have to click more times than this, it may be difficult to find information or it may even feel confusing. This also makes those Google crawlers or spiders be able to find your information much easier, which helps it to show up higher in search results.

It is also important to have a header that includes clickable links to your main categories on your site. This header should stay the same no matter what page of the site you are viewing. These headers are the types of menus that optimize SEO. Other menus like side menus or drop down menus do not help SEO at all, even if they may look nice on your site.

You can also use internal links on your web page. When you use internal links, it will help to make more traffic visit multiple pages on your site instead of just the one they initially set out to view. It will also show Google that your pages are being linked to, which is again the most important factor in how Google ranks you in their search engine results. Yes, it even counts when you link to your own information!

These ways of structuring your site are important to think about whether you are just now building your page or if you are rearranging your site in order to have better SEO. If you follow these structure tips, your search engine rankings are sure to be higher than they would be otherwise.

Next let's look into how to make Google notice your keywords. You use many words in your article, so how does Google know which ones to pick up as keywords for your SEO? Well, you will need to know about keyword placement in order to help yourself in this area. It is helpful if you put a keyword in your first paragraph and in your last paragraph in order for Google to notice them. You can also pay attention to your keyword density. This is the percentage of keywords you use in comparison to the rest of the words you use in your article. The best keyword density is typically between one and three percent. This allows Google to notice your keywords, but keeps your writing readable for your site visitors at the same time.

Now that we have covered how you can get your website to show up well in Google rankings, let's figure out how you can get people to actually click on the link to your site. We have already mentioned some things that can help in this area. First, make sure that you have a strong, intriguing title tag. This is what people pay the most attention to, so if it is a good title, more people are likely to click on your site in their Google search.

Next, you will need to make sure that your URL is set up nicely. You want your URL to be both readable and in a logical order. This is something that may look at in their google result as well, so it is important for it to be something that looks relevant and of high quality.

Site Speed is important for your Google ranking as well. Of course, site speed is important to your viewers. This allows viewers to enjoy your site and to possibly, and hopefully, even link to it. Why is it important to Google, though? Well, this again goes back to those crawlers or spiders. The faster your site is, the faster the crawlers or spiders can look through the information. The more information they find, the higher you will show up in the Google rankings, which in turn optimizes your SEO.

Next we will look into duplicate content versus original content. Original content helps your SEO and duplicate content hurts your SEO. This is because if you have the same information as another site or extremely similar information to another site, Google does not really know which one to rank above or below the other one. If you have completely original content, Google does not have a problem separating you from other results. This will avoid you having to have potentially lower SEO results for a great page just because someone else has a page with similar information.

Usability is an important thing to keep in mind when trying to optimize your SEO as well. It's kind of difficult to see why SEO and usability are related, since usability is something that is experienced by visitors after they have already found and gotten to your web page. However, it truly is important. It's important because good usability keeps people coming back to your site and even may make people refer you or link to your content. These things will not happen if your site is difficult to use. Because of this, if your site is easier to use, it will positively affect your SEO.

As we mentioned earlier in the article, mobile support is very important to SEO as well. This is because most people today browse the internet on their smartphones. This makes your web page useless if they are not able to view it from their mobile devices. Google knows this as well and they take this into account when ranking you in the search engine results.

Google not only rates your site with online algorithms and spiders and crawlers, but with human raters as well. These raters look at your web pages and judge them based on Google's search quality guidelines. These guidelines do update, so it is important to stay on top of what they are so that you can optimize your SEO with these human raters as well as the online ones. There are over 10,000 of these people who rate search engine results around the world. Google contracts with them to have their help in their ranking system. These raters are given words or phrases to search, and then they rate and rank the results that show up. This allows Google to ensure that real people are happy with the results that their computers are creating, and allows them to change the results if the real people are not happy with them.

One important thing to think about when looking into Google's search quality guidelines and human ranking team is that they look not only into your website and the information you have on it, but also into you as the author or creator of the site. This makes it more important than ever for you to have an "about me" section on your website. If you do not have this section about yourself or if it does not make you seem both credible and interesting, your SEO results may fall because of it.

This helps Google to make sure that authors and creators of sites are credible. This helps them with the amount of fake news that has been spreading online lately. Google wants to spread true information, and this is part of their way to do so.

Another thing that these human raters check for is that sites actually have interesting and useful information that relates to the word or phrase being searched for. Many sites today just write with many keywords to make their page show up in Google without making their information beneficial at all. Google discovered this and is fixing that problem with their search quality guidelines and human raters.

These are just a couple of the Google search quality guidelines. Make sure to stay up to date on these guidelines to ensure that your web page has optimal SEO, because the guidelines do seem to change frequently.

Next, let's look into readability. This is one of those topics that is again difficult to see affecting SEO because it is something that users experience after they actually get to your site, not when they are choosing it from search engine results. However, just like the usability, readability keeps visitors coming back to your site. It may make them refer others to your site or may make them even link to your site in their own pages.

SEO also works very well with content marketing. Content marketing is making sure you have the right content on your site for the type of users you want to attract. It is made up of a target audience, valuable content, and promotion through things like ads. All of these tactics bring traffic to your site, which in turn betters your SEO. They also make your site more useful and usable, which again helps your SEO.

Google also uses something featured snippets. These are the results that they choose to feature in small amounts at the top of the search result page. If you get featured in these snippets, it can help your SEO and cause you to have significantly more traffic. Let's look into how you can get your page featured in these snippets.

First, you need to figure out which searches make Google snippets show up, as not all searches do this. Sometimes, they show up when the user enters a question into the search bar. Making sure your page comes up from searching a question that your site answers may be able to get you into the snippets section. To decide what questions to ask, think about your audience. What types of questions do you think they have?

We could easily say "Wow" about how much of a difference keywords make and how many different things go into your Google search result rankings. Let's make a checklist of things you should do or add in order to see your site show up toward the top of the page in search engine results.

- Use well-researched and effective keywords
- Pay attention to keyword placement and density
- Use title tags
- Have a clear, structures URL
- Put your site menu in your header
- Give your site a logical structure
- Pay attention to your site load speed
- Make sure you are not displaying duplicate content- from your site or another site
- Make sure your site is usable and readable
- Pay attention to mobile friendliness
- Stay up to date on Google's search quality guidelines
- Write strong content, not just keywords
- Consider using content marketing
- Try to get featured in Google snippets by using question keywords

If you do these things, your SEO should be better than ever. These tips will help you to get to the top few spots in Google search results. They will increase the traffic to your site therefore boosting your business or web page. Make sure you know the information in this chapter well and refer back to it as you are creating or restructuring your site. These tips and tricks and things that are easy to do, but come with a big reward.

# Chapter Three: Link Building– How to Rank Extremely High on Google

So far in this book, we have mentioned many ways in which you can optimize your SEO and make your web page show up higher in the Google search results. Do you remember, though, what the very best way to raise your search engine result ranking was? That's right, the best way to raise your rank in the search results is through links. Both having links to strong content and being linked to from other websites helps your SEO greatly. In this chapter, we are going to look into something called link building. We will talk about what link building is exactly, a dirty little secret that no one tells you about link building, how to use link building and how not to use it, and more.

First, let's look into what link building really is. Link building is the process that you use to get other websites and their authors to link to your page. Remember, this is the factor that Google gives the most power to when ranking you in their search engine results, so it really is very important if you want your SEO to be successful. Building links both brings new visitors to your site and therefore adds to your traffic, and also adds to your level of authority when Google looks into your page. It shows that other people on the internet like your information and that they trust you. It shows that your content is beneficial, useful, and readable. It proves to Google that you probably have many of the important SEO factors, because people would not link to you if you did not have these.

It is important to know that there are two ways to get people to link to your site and that they are definitely not equal in their benefits. The first way that you can get linked to is to purchase backlinks. You can go online and pay a person or company to link to your site. This process is not ideal and should be avoided if possible. This can make you have links to your site that are from low quality places. It can even get your site blocked or banned for using this method of backlinking. This is because Google wants their results to actually be useful and have real authority, not authority that you can purchase on the internet.

The way that you should get people to link to your site is called the natural way. This process is difficult and it takes time and maybe even a little bit of luck, but it helps your SEO greatly so it is very worth it.

It is also important to note that even though you are getting links naturally, not all links are as helpful as others. Links give you better credibility when they are put in a larger website that has great SEO. If you get linked to in a site like National Geographic, for example, this would be huge. Not only does National Geographic have a huge following and list of readers that would possibly click on your link and be turned into your traffic, but they are also a big, trustable source in the eyes of Google. When Google sees you linked to popular or well-visited websites, they give you a higher ranking in their search results that if you were linked to in a smaller, less visited page.

Think about if instead of being linked to in National Geographic, you were linked to in your cousin's parenting blog that has about twelve trusted followers. This would cause much less traffic to visit your site through clicking the link, if any at all. Your cousin's blog also isn't a source that Google knows as credible, so it would not heighten your SEO results even close to as much.

It is important to remember, however, that any natural link is better than nothing. These links are still factored into your Google rankings. Even if it just a link from a small business in your area, it is much better than having no links at all in terms of your SEO.

So, link building is very important as you can see. It is important because it brings new visitors to your site. It is also important because it improves your credibility in the eyes of Google, which in turn allows you and your site to rank higher within their billions of results.

Next, let's look into a dirty little secret that typically no one would tell you about link building. We are telling you this because we want you to succeed, so we are giving you every piece of information that we have and every piece of knowledge that you will need in order to be extremely successful with your SEO. The big secret in link building is that Google is watching what you are trying to do. They are watching you and they are trying to stop you. Google knows that people have come up with strategies to be linked to in another peoples' content. This is not something they want. They want their results to be completely natural and they do not want you to have control over their systems. Because of this, pay attention to the tools and tricks that Google knows about and avoid them. For example, buying links actually used to work until Google found out and made it a process that you want to avoid at all costs. Pay attention to Google and what they are doing at the time. This changes all the time, so you will need to search often to stay updated.

Next, let's look into a linking tool called anchor text. When you put a link in your web page, you can decide if you want that link to simply show the URL of the source or if you want it to appear as something else that can be clicked on. You can make any words a clickable link with this tool. Anchor text allows you to put links in your content without losing its readability. It also is an easy way to tell people what they link is about, as well as an easy way to give them the site you are referring to just as they are reading about it and actually need it. Anchor text also looks much more professional that a clickable link that displays an entire URL in the middle of your web page content.

Anchor text also helps your SEO. The words that you choose to use for your clickable link tell Google what the content of the link is about. They use the words that you use for the link in order to decide what the content of the link actually is without ever needing to go to the linked site.

Anchor text also has the ability to show up at the end of a link's URL. When the text shows up here, it allows the URL to show what the content of the link is. Google can use this information to tell what the linked site is about as well.

There are six different types of anchor text that you can use or that you want others to use when linking to your site. Let's look into these six types of anchor text now.

- Exact-Match: This type of anchor text displays the exact same keyword that is used for the page that is being linked to. This ensures that it tells the reader what the link will be about.
- Partial-Match: This includes words that are similar to the keyword on the page being linked to, but not the exact same word or phrase. It still shows what the site will be about, however, just not in such an exact and precise way.
- Branded: This type of anchor text shows the name of the site or brand that is being linked to.
- Naked Link: This is simply using the URL and not choosing a specific word or phrase.
- Generic: This type of anchor text would say something along the lines of "click here".
- Images: The source for images that are sites are typically put in anchor text fashion, allowing readers to click on the links to see where the photo came from and allowing for the writers to give credit to the photographers.

When you are using anchor text, there are some important things to remember, This does not necessarily benefit your SEO, but it benefits the link that you are using and that person's SEO. If you benefit another person's SEO, they may want to help you as well. Because of this and just because it is the kind thing to do, you should make sure that your anchor text is made in the best way possible to allow it to get as many clicks as possible.

To make the best anchor text, make sure that it is a word or short phrase. If the phrase you use for the anchor text is too long, it may not look professional, may decrease readability, or may make less people actually go through and click on the link. You also need to make sure that the content you are linking to is relevant and useful. Random anchor text links to unrelated or unhelpful sites will only decrease the user approval rate of your own site, which in turn would hurt your SEO.

It can also be a good idea to consider not using a person's keyword when linking to their article. If people continually link to your web page with the same exact keyword, Google may notice this and they may think that you bought the links. Of course, this would not be natural link building so it would hurt your SEO greatly.

Now that we have learned all about links, what they are, what they do, and why they are important, let's look into how you can start link building and getting other people on the internet to link to your site. We will start by looking into some beginner strategies in the link building field.

One of the easiest link building strategies is to simply ask people you know if they could link to your site on their web page. You can ask family members or friends who have a blog or you could even ask local businesses that are in a related field to your content. You need to be a little bit careful with this strategy, because you only want related and relevant sites to link to your content. If your website is for selling crocheted items, you probably don't want links from a dentist office in an article that talks about taking care of your teeth, for example.

If your website is for a business, another thing that you can do to get a link is to list yourself on the Better Business Bureau. When you do this, the website will show a link to your site. This is an expensive way to get just one link, but it's a strategy to start with and a Better Business Bureau listing may even help your business anyway.

Also consider following along with other blogs that are similar to your website or your content. If you comment on their blogs often, they may start to notice you. They may then check out your page and they may like it and someday even decide to link to it. This is not a way that has guaranteed results, but it is a beginner strategy that is definitely at least worth a try.

If your website is a blog, you can also submit it to something called a blog directory. You can find these online and submit your blog/s link to them. This will help people who are looking for a blog like yours find you. It may also help people with similar bogs why can link build with you find you.

If you have a business, you can do the same but look for something called company directories instead of blog directories. This would again help people who are looking for a business like yours to find you online and would count as a link in the eyes of Google.

Another thing that you can try is reaching out to the people and the sites that you link to. If you link to someone else, they may feel thankful and want to repay the favor by linking to your site. This is again not a reliable way to do link building, but it is at least worth a shot since writing a simple email does not take long at all.

Let's look into some middle-level link building strategies next. If you are a business and you already have customers, you can ask them to review you or to link to you online if they have a place to do so from. This is intermediate because you need to already have customers so you cannot really be brand new to your business and use this technique.

You could also consider sending whatever you make or sell to a blogger for free, and asking them to write a review in return. If your product goes to a blogger that has good SEO and a well-established following, it will be a link that will help your Google rankings for sure.

You can even consider contributing to sites like Wikipedia. Wikipedia is used often so it is a reliable and useful source to get a link from. It can also be edited by anyone, including you. This means that you can go onto Wikipedia, find a related topic to your site, and then you can actually link to yourself.

Next let's look into a few higher-level link building strategies. One thing that you can do is be the first person online to cover a topic or a news story. This is tricky because there are so many people posting online, but if you are truly the first poster you will likely get linked to from most of the posters that follow you.

You could also consider buying websites that already exist and have a good follower base. This would mean you would need to run two websites, but you can use your newly purchased site to link to the one that you want to raise in the search engine result rankings.

Next you could look into other sites and find one that is missing exactly what you have. You could then reach out to the owner of the site and point out what they are missing. You could show them that you have everything they need and they may think about linking to your site. Make sure that you are kind and come across as helpful in this process so that you do not upset the person you are reaching out to.

We have covered a lot of information on link building. We talked about what link building is and why it is so important. We looked into how you can get links, strategies that actually work for each experience level, and what you should avoid when trying to get linked to. We talked all about anchor text why it is important, and how to use it. We looked into link outreach and how to do it kindly and correctly. With this information, you will be able to be linked to in many ways and significantly boost your SEO. Remember this information and the tips we have shared in this chapter and you are sure to find success with link building.

# Chapter Four: Social Media and SEO

In this next chapter, we are going to look into how exactly social media can affect your SEO. Social media is a fairly new thing that has been continuing to develop over the last decade, but it is something that almost every person uses today. Most people even spend time on it every single day of their life. If something has that big of an impact on society, it must be able to affect your search engine optimization.

The history of SEO and social media has been somewhat rocky. In the early days of social media, it was clear that it was a great tool for SEO. Then, in 2014, Twitter actually blocked Google from being able to use their analytics. Because of this, the importance of SEO and social media dies down quite a bit. Now, however, social media is extremely important to SEO again.

First, let's look into why social media is important to SEO. Google has started to realize that people love social media sites like Facebook, Twitter, and other sites. Because of this, they have been showing up in Google search results more and more. Google actually now considers these sites to be within their top one hundred sites to provide search results from. If Google puts this much weight on results coming from social media sites, it must impact your site's rankings somehow.

Let's figure out how this affects your site. First, SEO is for Google and social media is for interacting with the visitors of your site. Both are important, and both are actually related to each other as well. When you interact with the people from your site on a personal level, you are forming more of a relationship with them. This will make them want to read your information more often, which in turn will make you have more site traffic.

People are more likely to share the things that they love on social media than on other parts of the internet, because this is just how people live and interact in today's society. Because of this, your followers may share either your social media page or your actual website with the people they love on social media sites like Facebook or Twitter. If they do this, you will get new site visitors as well as more traffic from the older ones.

One of the ways that social media can help you the most is through content promotion. You can share any and all of the articles that you want to share with your followers. You do not need to worry about them needing to find your article through Google or SEO in this manner, but the extra traffic you receive of course still benefits your SEO anyway without much effort from you.

Social media also helps your brand awareness. When people are more aware of your company, blog, r web page, then more people will visit your site. This again helps your SEO. You can make people more aware of your site through social media because so many people are mindlessly scrolling through there already.

It is also important to know that your posts on social media are actually treated the same way that a web page is treated in the results of Google searches. This means that you should give as much importance to your social media posts as you do to your website, because they could be the things that show up in the Google search results first.

Let's look into some ways that you can use Facebook specifically to bring new visitors and traffic to your actual site. Facebook has something called a total count. When you share a post, this is the total number of likes, comments, and shares that your post receives. This exact number plays a huge role in where your post shows up in Google search result rankings. If your total number is high, your post has a much better chance at being seen in Google search results than if your total number was low.

Facebook is also a good link building tool. This is because people that you do not know will see the information that you share on your page without you even having to market to them. This may make some of your followers link to your content without you even putting in an effort to build links. This makes Facebook and great and easy tool that you can use to potentially raise your SEO.

Most of the time, Facebook is not a professional environment. Because of this, it is important for you to remember that even though it is just Facebook you still need to keep your content professional. This is important because again, your social media posts can show up in Google results. If an unprofessional post shows up on Google instead of your actual page, your SEO will be significantly lowered from the lack of site visits that you will receive.

Twitter now allows Google to see and use their information and the information posted to their sites by users again, so it is again a great tool to use for SEO. On Twitter, you need a lot of followers to show up in Google results. To get a large number of followers, try following a large amount of people. If you follow them, they are pretty likely to at least click on your page to check you out. If they like you and your page, they may even follow you back.

If you put high quality content on Twitter, you can use hashtags to help your intended audience to find your post. Make sure that your quality is good and that the content matches with what the hashtag says, though, so that your posts do not come across as spam.

It is also important that on Twitter, you fill out your biography section and that you fill it out in an accurate and exciting way. This will make more people interested in what you have to say because they will be interested in you as well. You should also put a link to your website in your biography section to help the people that like your tweets reach your actual page and give you even more traffic than you already have at the time.

There are other sites that can help your SEO as well. YouTube, for example, is a great one. YouTube is owned by Google, so their results show up high more times than not. Instagram, LinkedIn, and Pinterest can all be good SEO tools to use as well.

Next, let's look into something called social media analytics. Social media analytics are sites and tools that you can use to tell you how well you are performing on social media. They can tell you how many people are seeing your posts, interacting with it, and how to improve these numbers. They can tell you the best times of day to post to your specific group of followers as well as the posts that they enjoyed the most. This will help you to know your follower base well and understand what they want. You can then consider giving them more of what they want and less of what they do not want. This helps your social media followers to thoroughly enjoy their interactions with you and makes them much more likely to share your page and site with their followers, families, and friends.

Sprout Social is a good social media analytics tool. It can be tried for free for thirty days and then costs 99 dollars every year. It works with Facebook, Twitter, Instagram, and LinkedIn. This tool is nice because it allows you to see all of your social media accounts from different platforms all in one place. This can save you a lot of time and effort compared to having a separate analytic tool for every social media site that you have an account with.

Buzzsumo is a good tool to use as well. This tool does not look into your social media accounts. Instead it finds your actual website content on different social media platforms. It then tells you how these articles or this content is doing in different areas of the internet. This can be very helpful if you are looking into an article and not a social media account. Buzzsumo searches Facebook, Twitter,

Instagram, LinkedIn, and Pinterest. It also costs 99 dollars for every year that it is used.

Overall, it is easy to see that social media plays a huge role in your SEO and simply how people view and interact with the information that you post online, either on your social media accounts or on your website. Let's make a list of the things that you need to remember about social media and SEO.

- Social media post show up in Google results
- Social media sites increase viewer interactions
- Social media gains traffic for your actual site
- Make sure to have accurate and interesting social media biographies
- Facebook, Twitter, Instagram, LinkedIn, YouTube, and Pinterest can all affect SEO
- Social media analytic tools can help you manage your social media accounts and can help maximize the benefits coming from them

With this information and the tips and tricks that we shared in this chapter, you have every piece of information that you need in order to make your social media sites optimize your SEO.

# Chapter Five: Web Analytics in a Nutshell- How to Measure Success

In the last chapter we touched on social media analytics, but in this chapter we are going to look into complete web analytics. We will talk about what Google Analytics is and why it is a good tool to use as well as how to use Google Analytics. We will talk about acquisition, organic search reports, segments, and other common web analytic terms. We will also look into call tracking, a powerful analytics tool for every business, as well as other web analytics tools.

First, let's figure out what Google Analytics is exactly. Google Analytics is a tool that tells you about the traffic that visits your site. It is similar to the social media analytic tools that we talked about above, but it simply works with your web page instead of your social media accounts.

Now let's look into why exactly you should be using Google Analytics to help optimize your SEO. The first reason why you should use this tool is because it is free. If something helps your SEO and does not cost you any money at all to use, why would you not give it a try? The fact that Google Analytics is free is a really great deal. Think back to the social media analytics tools that we talked about in the last chapter, for example. Both of them cost 99 dollars every single year that you use them. One came with one free month, but that is nowhere near as good of a deal as being a free tool for your entire lifetime. Since this tool does not cost you anything, you might as well at least give it a try.

The second reason why you should use this tool is because it is made by Google. Google is the company that created the tool, runs the tool, and provides you with your results. Why is this so important? Because Google is the exact company that you want your company to look good for. If this tool analyzes your website with Google's standards, it will surely raise your search result rankings in their own search engine. If you use an optimization tool made by the company who you are ultimately trying to impress, it is sure to be helpful.

Google Analytics is also a good tool to use simply because it works. It provides you with the results you are looking for when you use a web analytics tool. It gives you information about your site and the type of people who are viewing it. It can tell you your peak days and your peak hours as well as where your site is being accessed from on the internet. This information is very useful to figuring out how to improve your SEO, so you might as well take advantage of it.

Now that we know what Google Analytics is and why you should use it, let's look into how it works. It is important for you to understand how your SEO optimization tools work for a few reasons. The first reason why you should be aware of this information is so you can trust the tool. If you know how it works, you know that the information it provides is accurate and that its findings are typically very complete. You should also know how it works so that you can understand where the tool gets its results. If you understand how the tool gets the results that it gives you, you will be able to understand how to implement them better.

So, how exactly does the Google Analytics tool work? First, it works through the use of coding techniques. The URL to your website already uses coding, but Google Analytics puts many more codes into this as well. They also put more tracking codes into the coding inside the content of your web page. This cannot be seen by your site visitors so it does not affect your usability or readability. It does, however, track everything that the visitors of your site do. It even looks into the attributes of your site visitors and records them as well. These attributes include things like the gender, age, and even the interests of the people who view your web page.

Once the codes collect this information, they send it over to the Google Analytics page to be analyzed. They look into actions that every user does when they visit your site, how long each visitor spends in time on each part of your web page, how many times each separate page is viewed, how many buttons are clicked, how many times each video is viewed, and more. You can use this information to see what on your website is working well and what is viewed often by the visitors of your site, as well as what may not be going as well and what may not be being viewed very often at all.

Next, let's look into the information that Google Analytics provides back to you and how you can use it to benefit your site as well as your search engine optimization. The types of information that Google provides you with through the use of this tool are divided up into two separate categories.

The first of these two categories is User Acquisition Data. This information is all about the people who view your site and it is the information that Google has found out about them before they clicked on your site at all. It may tell you how old your viewers are, what gender they are, or what they like and what they dislike. User Acquisition Data can also tell you how these visitors got to your site in the first place. This data can tell you if the viewers clicked on a google result or if they came over through a link in a Facebook post.

This information is extremely helpful. It can help you to know what type of people are viewing your site. If you know what types of people you are writing to, you can consider catering your page more toward them instead of toward people who are not yet interested in your page. It is also extremely helpful to know how people are getting to your site. If people are mostly coming through Google search results, then you know that your SEO is in great shape. If no one is coming from Google searches at all, you know that your SEO probably needs a little help. If you see that many visitors are coming from Facebook posts, you can make sure you update your Facebook often to continue to allow more new site visitors to find you online, and so on.

The second of these two important categories of Google Analytics results is something called User Behavior Data. Instead of showing what your site visitors are like before getting to your site and telling you how they get to your site like User Acquisition Data, this category of information tells you all about what your site visitors do once they are already on your web page.

One of the first things that this tool can tell you about the people on your page is how long they stay on your page. This can tell you if people are enjoying your content or not. If most site visitors are only spending a few seconds on each of your pages, you may have some work to do to make your site more enjoyable If people spend many minutes on one particular page, you know that that is the type of content that they are looking for and the type of thing that they enjoy reading, listening to, watching, etc.

The tool can also tell you which page your visitors see first and which page they see last. This can help to show you which page your links are bringing visitors to and if this is a good first page to see or a bad first page to see. If it's the only page they view, it may not be the best first page. If they continue to click through all of your pages until the end, this may be a great sign. If people commonly stop viewing your content on a certain middle page, this may alert you to some sort of problem that they do not enjoy as well.

This tool can even tell you the order in which site visitors view your pages. This may be able to help you rank the interest levels of your different pages according to your specific group of viewers that you have for your web page.

User Behavior Data is interesting because it is an easy thing for you to change. You can look at the information that this tool gives you and adjust your site accordingly. If you do this, it is likely that you will quickly see results. It is much more difficult to change the results of your User Acquisition Data than it is to change your User Behavior Data.

The next thing that we are going to look into on the topic of web analytics and Google Analytics is something called organic search reports. Before we start going too deep into these details, let's learn what organic search results really are. First, it is important to understand that your website cans how up in Google search results naturally through good use of SEO tactics, or it can show up as a paid ad. Paid ad are not organic search results. Anything that appears naturally through SEO and is not paid for at all is considered an organic search result.

When you are using web analytic tools like Google Analytics, you should really be looking into your organic search results. You already know that paid ads will bring viewers to your site, but the long term goal is typically to get people to come to your site naturally without you having to pay for ads. In Google Analytics, you can look for just organic search report, which will show you how well your site is doing from a natural viewpoint. It will take out any type of data that comes through advertisements of any kind. When you view your website's organic search reports, you will be able to see what you need to do to improve your SEO if anything. It will help you to better understand the success of your website even if you have used paid advertisements in the past to promote yourself online. This tool will help you to see straight past those results so you can make sure that you have a great SEO that does the hard work for you.

We are now going to look into segments in regards to web analytics and Google Analytics. Segmentation in web analytics is when you look at the visitors that are coming to your site and then you divide them into different groups, or different segments. These segments could be something like first time visitors and returning visitors, for example. These segments help you to learn more about the people that are viewing and interacting with your site. They help you to see and understand what types of people are doing what types of things on your website.

When you understand the visitors that come to your site, you can better understand what they are looking to gain from your work. This can help you to format your site and frame your content to fit the needs of all of the types of people that you are virtually working for and working with.

There are many different types of segments that you can search for using Google analytics and other web analytic tools. One of these segments would be demographics. It can help you to understand where your readers are from and what areas of the world are interacting in which ways.

It may also help to do segments based on technology. This can help you to understand how many people are viewing your site from their smartphone and how many people are viewing your site from their laptop computer. You can then look into whether people seem to enjoy your site more in either of these settings or if they interact with your site more in either of these settings. This can then tell you if your site needs extra work in its mobile friendliness or if you should work more on how it looks when it is viewed from a computer screen.

You can also segment your viewers based on their behaviors. This can tell you if a lot of your views and interactions are coming from the same people over and over again or if your site following is made up of a large amount of people that do not visit your site very often at all. It can also tell you if the people who visit often interact more or if the new viewers interact more with the things that are on your web page.

Looking into the date that the people visited your site for the first time can be interesting as well. Are all of your visitors from when your site was made six months ago? If so, you may need to attract some new viewers. Did half of your followers show up on a random day in February? If so, look back to what you did that day in terms of marketing and definitely consider doing something similar to it again and again.

It may be helpful to look into your site visitors in groups based on how they found you online as well. This can help you to see if the people that mainly interact with your page content come from social media links or from Google search results. This can help you to determine if your site may need help in either of these two areas.

Enhanced Ecommerce can be a helpful way to segment site visitors as well. It can help you to see, if your site has things for sale, which of your interactions are coming from people who often purchase from you and which are coming from people who simply browse your site without ever making any purchases.

Now that we have looked into web analytics and specifically Google Analytics in such great detail, let's do a quick recap together. We talked about what Google Analytics is, why it is important, and how to use it. We looked into acquisition, organic search reports, and segments. Next, let's review some of the new web analytic terms that we have learned so far over the course of this chapter.

Acquisition: This is how people find your site. It's the way they reach your content, whether through Google search results, social media posts, links, or even just typing in your complete URL for your site.

Organic Search Report: This is a report that you can make through Google Analytics. It includes only your natural search results and does not include any visitors that come from clicking on paid advertisements.

Segments: When looking at web analytics, segments are groups that you can use to divide the visitors of your site by attributes like age, gender, site behaviors, and even their purchase history and many more.

Next, let's look into another important thing in web analytics called Call Tracking. Have you ever searched for a business because you needed to call them, and then been able to simply click on their phone number to complete the call? This information can be tracked with Google Analytics, and it is very important that you choose to take advantage of this. This is important because typically, people do not think about SEO when they receive phone calls. However, if you have a strong SEO and your phone number appears at the top of the result page, you are much more likely to get a phone call from someone searching on Google which of course can lead to more business for you. It is important to look into this information in Google Analytics so you know if it is working or if it is something that you need to improve on.

Finally, let's look into what types of web analytic tools are available online today. Of course, we already know about Google Analytics. This free told should definitely be used, but if you are looking for more than what Google Analytics offers, you may want to consider using a paid tool as well.

There are many different web analytic tools out there. It is up to you to decide which tool will benefit your business to the very best. The first web analytics tool that we will look into is called Adobe Analytics. It is easy to use and easy to understand, and it also provides real time data, not data that has been read hours ago in the past. This can be important when trying to optimize your SEO. It works very well, but it is extremely expensive. It costs many thousands of dollars every single moth if you want to use it. Because of this, it is really only a told that should be used by businesses that are already extremely rich and successful as well as businesses that know they will benefit from extensive web analytic help.

Angelfish Actual Metrics is a more middle ground product, but is still quite expensive as it adds up to over one thousand dollars each year that you need to pay to use its service. With Angelfish, you have the ability to measure the analytics of multiple sites at the same time, so it can be good for people that have more than one web page that they need to optimize. It also has the benefit of showing hidden visitors that google analytics does not have the ability to show to you.

If you are a beginner, Google Analytics is probably still the best place to start. This is because it is free so you are not wasting money if the web analytic tool you buy is something that is difficult to understand at first. Google Analytics also simply has most if not all of the features that beginners will want and need.

Overall, it is easy to see that web analytics are something that you really do need to know about when you are trying to optimize your SEO online. They help you to understand a lot more about the types of visitors that come to your site. They help you to see how people are finding your site, how much time they are spending on it, and how much they are interacting with you as well as many more helpful details. There are free web analytic tools as well as paid tools so there is a tool that is right for every type of web page and every different experience level.

Web analytics are important. We know that with this information, you will be able to understand them at least enough to start using them while trying to optimize your SEO. If you use web analytic tools in the ways that we have shared with you in this chapter, we are sure that your website and your following will benefit because of it.

# Chapter Six: Troubleshooting Common SEO Problems

Sometimes, optimizing your SEO can be a frustrating process. Things can go wrong and you can lose the results that you worked so hard for. You can do all of the necessary steps and still not see the results that you so badly want to see. Because this can be difficult and frustrating, we are going to help you learn about common problems with SEO as well as how to troubleshoot each of these tricky issues.

First, let's look into what to do if your site in not showing up at all in Google's search results. The best way to check if your site is showing up is to type in your exact URL into the search bar. This should bring up a clickable link to your web page. If it does not, then your site is not showing up at all in the Google search results.

How can you fix this? It seems like a very complicated issue, but it actually is something that you can fix. You will want to check your site's Google search performance. It is likely that you need to greatly improve your SEO as well as other aspects of your web page in order to allow it to show up in the rankings.

Another reason why your site could be not showing up in the Google search results is because it is too new. Google needs some time to process and rank new sites, so its possibly that your brand new site may not be visible in Google search results for a little while after you create it. If this is the problem, there is not much that you need to do to fix it. In fact, there really isn't anything that you could do to fix this even if you wanted to. In this circumstance, you would simply need to give Google time. If your site is set up well and your SEO is at least off to a good start, your web page will show up in Google search results soon enough.

Remember those crawlers and spiders that we keep going back to? They could be the reason why you are not showing up in Google searches as well. If these spiders and crawlers cannot access your site, Google may not be able to see enough information to accurately display you in their search results. In order to make sure that these crawlers and spiders can do their job, you need to make sure that your website is accessible, that it has a good site speed, and that your site and URL are structured well. If you do not do these things, then the spiders or crawlers will have a very difficult time viewing your site if they can at all, and because of this they will not bring very much information if any back to Google. This will cause you to either not rank at all in Google search results or cause you to rank extremely low.

It is actually even possible that you are blocking these crawlers or spiders from reaching your page, and you may not even know that you are doing this. Some blog and website making software and websites like WordPress, for example, has an option that will completely block crawlers or spiders. If you accidentally checked the box that tells WordPress or any other site to do this, you will need to uncheck the box to make sure that spiders and crawlers are always able to access your site. After all, we know that they are extremely important.

It could also mean that you need to work on your keywords if you do not show up from Google searches. If your keywords are not placed correctly or if the keyword density on your site is not optimal, this could greatly affect your results in Google. It could also mean that the keyword you are using is not generating the results that you want. If this is the case, you would need to research new keywords and pick one that will perform better for you on your site.

If none of these situations apply, check your website's coding. It is possible that when you set your site up or when someone set your site up for you, it accidentally got set up with a "no index" tag. This type of tag would make your website not show up at all in certain Google searches. Check with the person who made your website to see if they could have accidentally done this. If you made your website, look into your coding for signs that you may have made a little mistake in this area that caused these tags to be added. The good thing is that as soon as your no index tags are removed, your site should show right back up in your Google search results.

If all of these things look good on your site but you still are not seeing it show up in Google search results, try to figure out if Google could have possibly taken down your web page. Google takes down sites everyday. They do this both if the site does not meet the Google quality guidelines and if it for some reason contains untrue or illegal information. If your site has been removed from Google, you will probably need to reach out to see what it was that you did wrong on your site. When you figure out why exactly your site was removed, you can go ahead and fix that problem. This should make your web page show up in Google search results fairly quickly once again.

Now that we know what to do if your site is not showing up in Google search results at all, let's move a little farther forward. Next, we are going to look into what you should do if your website is not ranking in the results for your own business name. Obviously, this is a problem that you do not want to have. It means that when people know about your company and they want to find it, they will either not be able to find it at all or they will at the very least have an extremely difficult time finding it. This will definitely hurt your site traffic and it will also probably hurt your complete business as well.

The first thing to do when this problem arises is to make sure that you are not checking your Google search results from your own browser. If you are, Google may be showing you different results because they know that you own your website. This could make your website come up as the top result for you since Google knows you visit it often, and this may make you think your SEO is in great standing when in all reality it needs a lot of help. It could also do the opposite. Googling your own site from your own browser could make your web page not show up in the results at all, even if you are searching your business name. This is because Google is giving you results for what you search for, they know that you already have access to your own website and the information that it holds. Because of this, they are showing you new information.

To get around this feature in Google, you will want to open up an incognito, or secret, tab on your computer or mobile device. When you do this, Google will show you what everyone else in the world sees when they search the name of your site instead of just what Google shows to you. This can help you to get a clear and correct image of how Google portrays you to random searchers on the internet at this time. If you see what everyone else sees, you will probably find out that your web page actually is showing up in Google search results. You may even see many ways in which you can improve your SEO and get your rankings to move up higher on the list.

Another thing to look into if your site is not showing up when you search for your own company name is to check on your SEO tactics. Make sure that your keyword usage is in good shape. Make sure that your site is readable and usable. Make sure that it has a structure that actually makes sense. Look into your analytics and search for reasons why your website may not be going as well as you think it is going. If it is not showing up in very exact Google searches, it probably needs quite a bit of formatting help before it will be ready to be published again. If you follow the tips we have shared with you in this book, however, fixing your website should be a pretty quick and painless process.

Now that we have looked into what to do when you cannot find your website on Google in their search results, let's look into what you can do when you do find your website but it happens to be at a much worse ranking than it was when you checked in on it the week before. There are many reasons why you could see a Google ranking drop, let's look into what they are and what you can do if they happen to you and your website.

The first thing that could make your rankings drop significantly is if you receive a Google penalty. Google penalties happen when you do not follow along with the Google quality standards. You can tell that this is the problem with your site if you type in different searches with multiple different keywords, and your site is significantly lower than it used to be for every single search that you do. If you happen to find that you have received a Google penalty, first you should figure out why you received it. You can then go ahead and fix the problem. This should make your rankings go back up to where they used to be in just a little amount of time.

Your Google rankings could also drop when another search result, one of your competitors, moves ahead of you in the rankings. This can mean that they somehow improved their SEO to the point that they show up higher in the results than you do. This one is a little more difficult to come back form as it takes some time, but you will need to work on your SEO to once again surpass this competitor. Consider looking at the site of your competitor. What are they doing to improve their SEO? How are they tackling the ever important task of link building? It is obvious that what they are doing is working well, so you may even want to consider copying what they are doing. They are showing you that their tactics are giving them the results that you want and need, so you might as well try these tactics for yourself.

On Page issues can cause your site's ranking to drop as well. These problems could be something as simple as broken links. If your google search result rankings seem to be dropping from on page issues, consider carefully reviewing all of the content on your site as well as the features that your site has. If you can find an error, fixing it will probably help you to move back up to where you were and where you want to be in the search results.

Another reason why your search result rankings could have dropped is because there was a recent change to Google. Google has many updates and is constantly trying to improve. Because of this, they often change the algorithms that they use to rank search results as well. If you can find no reason why your site should be dropping based on how it looks or how your competition looks, check in with Google. If they have recently done an update, you will have found your issue. You can also try to stay ahead of Google updates as well. If you know when the updates are coming, you can adjust your site so that its ranking never actually gets to the point where it will drop.

The last reason why your site may drop that we are going to look into together is classed a Google Flux. This Google Flux is something that you have no control over. They are also unpredictable, so you will never be able to tell when they are going to happen. They make your site drop for no reason. Luckily, this is not a permanent drop and your site will be back at the ranking that it belongs in within a few days. If you can find no reasons for your site to drop based on your web page and based on your competitors, and you also see no signs of a Google update, it is probably a Google flux. Try not to worry and check back in a few days. Most likely, your search result rankings will be back to normal.

These are the most common problems that you may face that lead to your Google search result rankings dropping. When you see them, you can look back to this chapter so that you are able to help your rankings return to normal. With this information, you should be able to troubleshoot any search engine ranking issue that comes your way.

If you are still having a hard time with your SEO, however, you may just feel like you need some advice or help from a professional. Professional help is always a great thing to have, but of course it can be extremely expensive. Luckily, there is a tool that allows you to get free SEO help from a professional online.

This tool is a website called WiSEO. On this site, you can type in a question that has to do with any part of SEO. When the professionals on the website see your question, they will take the time to answer your question. They do not do this for money of course because their service is free. They do this simply to help you in your journey with SEO. They are a great resource to keep on hand.

Overall, with the information in this chapter, you should be able to solve any search result ranking that comes your way. If you come across a problem that you are not able to solve, you can always reach out to the experts at WiSEO for free, professional help.

# Chapter Seven: SEO for Local Business

Typically, your SEO helps your site to show up in search engine results from anywhere in the world. When you use local SEO, however, you can promote your site or your business to people who are near you. In this chapter we are going to learn all about local SEO. We will talk about why using SEO is important, how you can rank high with local SEO, and local SEO search ranking factors. We will discuss how exactly you can go about getting started with local SEO. We will learn about building citations and building reviews. We will also look into supercharging local SEO with photos and videos as well as a local SEO ranking checklist and other essential resources.

One important thing to note is that in order to use local SEO to its best ability, you need to have a proper physical address. If you do not have an address that you can publicly use for your site information, you will not get very much out of using local SEO. However, if you do not have a physical address that you can use in the area, you can still use some local SEO. In this case, you would simply need to write a lot of content about the area you want your readers to be from. If you do this, your result should still show up in Google's search results when people are looking for something in that specific area.

Now let's look into why exactly you should use local SEO. Local SEO is extremely important because it simply provides great results. It is a tool that can build your SEO quickly. It is also just another way to build your search engine optimization. If you've already done all of the tips and tricks we have talked about in this book so far and you want your website to still rank higher in Google's search results, local SEO has another new list of tips and tricks that can help you achieve this.

Local SEO is extra important if you are a small business owner with only one or a few in-person locations. It is important in this situation because you want your site to show up in the results of local searchers. If you have a plumbing company in Pittsburg, you probably do not care if you show up in the search results of people who are looking for plumbing in San Diego. You only really need to show up in local searches. In cases like this, you can focus mainly on local SEO tactics while you are building your site.

Now that we have looked into what local SEO is, why you should use it, and how to rank high with it, let's look into the local search ranking factors.

Knowing this information will again help you to improve your local SEO simply because you know the basis of what makes you rank high or low or somewhere in between.

One great tool to use in local SEO besides writing about your specific city of interest is writing about the towns that surround that city. People will drive away for things that they like or things that they want to experience. Because of this, if you also market to people who live in surrounding areas, you may get into their search results as well. If you have good content on your site that interests your visitors, they may choose you even over businesses that are physically closer to them.

Another really cool thing about local SEO is that it does not have to contain only online pieces to help it succeed. If you tell people in person about your business, they may go home and look up your website online. If you have a billboard or put up flyers, people may see your name and search for you specifically on Google. If you have customers that are happy with your services, they may tell their neighbors and local friends about you as well, which would once again lead to people looking you up online and bettering your SEO.

For local SEO, you will also want to do something called "Google My Business". This is a Google service that helps businesses to share their own details. It allows you to go onto Google's site and edit facts about your site or company. It will ask you to add all of your locations and to verify your business. This will allow your site to show up higher in the searches of local people because Google knows that your company is real. Google My Business also lets your customers log into its site and rate and review your business. If you have good reviews, your site will show up higher in local Google. If you have poor reviews, your site will show up lower in the search results. When you get reviews, you can even go a step further by responding to the comments that are left by your customers. You want to be very friendly in these comments. You also want to make sure that if you receive poor reviews you do not respond to the comments with a grudge or any other type of negative tone. If you get a good review, sincerely thank the person who left it. If you get a not so good review, sincerely try to help improve the negative experience the person had with your business. When you are interacting with customers online, Google suggests that you treat them like a friend. This well help to show that you care and will improve the way that local people see your business. Even if potential customers see bad reviews online, they will also see you trying to help solve the issues. This will help how people see you and your company which will in turn improve your business as well as your local SEO.

Another great tool for local SEO is Facebook. As we mentioned earlier in the book and as you probably already know, Facebook is everywhere. Not just is Facebook everywhere, but it seems like almost everyone in the world is on Facebook as well. Because of this, it is extremely important that your business is on Facebook and that it is represented well. Since people are on Facebook so much, it is pretty common for them to use it to find local businesses when they need something from them. They can do this by asking for recommendations or by simply searching for what they need in the search bar. If they have heard of your company before, they can look your Facebook page up to learn more about your business as well. Facebook also allows its users to review your business, so you can help your local SEO by responding to these comments nicely just like we talked about doing for the Google My Business reviews.

A simple way to optimize your local SEO is to just add your city and state to your title. When you do this, Google is able to tell easily which local searches you should be entered into. The title of your site is important in the factors that Google looks into for your SEO. Because of this, if your title includes both your business name and your city and state, it should show up well in the searches that you need it to show up in the most. This is also a good thing to do because it is so easy. It takes basically no time or effort and can make your Google search result ranking much better in the area where you want to advertise yourself the most.

You can also look into other local web directories. These are sites that list business information like yelp.com. These are good resources because they are simply another thing that can show your business in the local search results, and they can also have a link to your actual website. As we learned earlier, links like these are the best way to improve your SEO. The more directory sites you put your business information and site links into, the better your local SEO will be just because your name will be more visible in the search results and because of the link building that this does for you.

Let's look a little closer at these links that we have been talking so much about. In local SEO, the best links are people who refer your business or company on their site. This may be even better if the person referring you is also local and if they happen to have great local SEO. These links are still very powerful to your own SEO. They help your Google search results rankings greatly and direct people to your site from other places on the internet.

Even though you are working on getting local results here, you cannot forget about using the pieces of typical, widespread SEO. You still need to make sure the content of your site is as good as it can possibly be. It needs to be readable and usable so that it is able to be enjoyed by the visitors that come through. It needs to have a good structure and a well-made URL so that Google can read it and those spiders and crawlers can easily access your information.

In local SEO, you also need to remember keywords just as much as you need to do so in regular SEO. Make sure to use keywords both for describing your business as well as mentioning where you are from so that you are able to show up easily in the Google search results for both of these things.

You also need to remember that prominence is used in Google's local SEO decisions. When you have a perfect site with great SEO from every side, you may still be underneath that name brand company in your town that also has locations in every other town. If this happens, do not be discourages. This is simply one of the ways that Google chooses to rank results. If you keep working hard on your local SEO you may pass them up in the results someday. If not, remember that if people want the best option for the service or product that they need, they will probably look at and compare the top few choices. Because of this, you will likely still get a lot of business even if you lose the number one spot to a chain company location nearby.

After reading through all of these ways to rank high in local search results and the ranking factors of local SEO, you should be able to optimize the SEO of your local business site fairly easily. If you use all of these tips and tricks, we are sure that your local SEO will be in great shape.

Next, let's look into how to get started with local SEO. We already know what to do, but let's make a step by step game plan so that you can do this in as easy of a process as possible. We are here to help you the best we can!

1. Look at your title, does it include your city and state? If not, add it. This simple step will help you greatly in your local SEO success.

2. Make a Google My Business profile. Add and verify the information for your business. Bookmark this page so that you can come back to it to respond to any comments or reviews you happen to receive.

3. Make a Facebook page. Use this page to display business information, share posts that

may interest your intended viewers, and interact with your customers and potential customers. After all, most people are on Facebook today anyway. You may as well use it as a tool to share your business with them.

4. Add your business to local directory sites. The more times your business shows up in search results, the more times it will be seen. Plus, you can use this as an opportunity to link to your website as well.

5. Link Build! Ask other local sites and companies to link to your page and consider returning the favor and linking to their page as well. This is the one thing that makes a huge difference in your SEO.

6. Advertise around your city. If people see posters or billboards with your company name, they are likely to google it and look for your website.

7. Be friendly. Log back on to your Google My Business and Facebook profiles. Interact with the people you are reviewing you in kind and helpful ways.

8. Make sure your address is listed on your site.

9. Look at your website. Make sure the content is relevant. See that your site is readable and usable overall. Look at your keyword

placement and density. Look back to all of our regular SEO tactics and put them to use as well.

With these nine tips, you should not only be able to get started with local SEO, but you should be able to excel in this area as well. We hope this information causes your local Google search result rankings to skyrocket and that this leads to more business for your local company as well.

Now that we know how to use and benefit from local SEO, let's learn about something called citation building. First, it is important to know and understand that a citation is any type of mention of your business on the internet. These can be mentions of the name of your business, your address, your phone number, or any combination of the three of these pieces of information. A complete citation is called a NAP. NAP stands for name, address, and phone number. When a citation has all of your information because of the NAP, people online can find your business very easily either online or even in person.

The cool thing about citations is that even if they do not link back to your business's website, Google stills treats them the same way that they would treat a link. Remember how important links are? Because they are so important, this is a hugely helpful tool in local SEO. The more times your NAP, or really any part of your business, shows upon the internet, the higher it ranks in the Google search result rankings. Some of these citations can even include links to your website. This would make an even more powerful SEO boost for your company site.

There are two different types of citations in local SEO. One type of these is called a structured citation. These are from local directory sites like yelp.com that we mentioned earlier in this chapter. They can also be from sites like Facebook.

Unstructured citations are any other types of sites that show your business information but are not necessarily a listing for your company. These could include things like when your business is mentioned and reviewed in a blog and the writer includes your information so that people can try out your business as well.

Both of these types of citations help to verify your business to google and their search engine results team. It shows that your business is real because it is being mentioned in multiple different places on the internet by many different people. It also adds to your prominence level since you are mentioned more times online overall.

One thing that you really need to be careful about when it comes to citations is that your different citations round the web are consistent. They all need to have the correct information, so this should make them each have the same information as well. If the sites have incorrect or different information, this not only confuses your potential clients, but it hurts your local SEO as well.

Now that we have looked into building citations, how to do it, and why it is helpful, let's look into building something else. Next we are going to talk about building reviews, how you can build them, and why it is important to do so.

As we already know, reviews are comments from people who have used your products or services in real life. They are the honest opinions of your customers. They can be great, horrible, or somewhere in between. Reviews are made so that people know what they are getting before they decide to pay for your product or for your service. They ensure that people are getting high quality experiences from what they purchase as well, since if the products or services are bad someone is sure to tell the world about it soon enough.

The more good reviews you have, the better you show up in Google's search results rankings. This is why it is important for you to build up your reviews. Working on building reviews can be a fast way to boost your local SEO.

Next, let's look into how we can boost our reviews. The first way that we can boost reviews is pretty simple. When people visit our business, we can ask them to go online and review their experience with our products or services. If you ask a person to review you, they may actually do it. Of course it never hurts to ask someone for a favor, so this is any easy step that you might as well take to help your SEO improve at the local level.

Another thing that you can do to encourage reviews is to place signs inside your business that encourage people to review their experience online. This eliminates you having to ask every customer for reviews. It also helps customers to notice that a simple review is something that would really help your business in a concrete way.

You could also consider getting the email addresses of your customers when they pay at your business. If you do this, you can send them an email after asking them how their service was and asking them if they could please review you online. You could even provide a link in the email that the customer could click on in order to be brought to a site that they can leave a quick review on.

You could even try offering an incentive for the people that choose to leave a review. You could put their name into a monthly drawing or even give them a coupon for a percentage or a dollar amount off of their next service.

With these tips, you should be able to continue to get more reviews. The more reviews you get, the better your local SEO looks. Even if asking for reviews is not your favorite thing to do, remember that it is making a huge difference in your SEO.

There are a couple other things that we have not yet mentioned that make a huge difference in local SEO. The first of these two things is photos. When your site includes pictures, people are more likely to notice your business. Pictures are the main thing that is seen on social media today and it's easy to notice and recognize right away. If you have photos online, people will notice and interact with your content much more than if you did not have photos on your site. Because of this, something as simple as a picture of your storefront can benefit your local SEO in big ways.

Videos are the second of these two simple but strong tools. Videos are popular right now and most people like to watch them when they are surfing the web or scrolling through social media. Watching a video takes less effort than reading or researching, so viewers are more likely to learn all about your business in this fashion than they are to click onto your site and read through all of the pages. Because of these factors, videos can really supercharge local SEO.

In this chapter, we have learned all about local SEO. We have learned that it is just like SEO but for local searches and we have discussed why it is so important to use it. We have learned the ranking factors for local SEO as well as how to rank high with it. We created a list together of how to start this process, talked through citations, reviews, and even the great benefits of citations and reviews. After reading all of this information, you should be able to have great success with your local SEO.

# Chapter Eight: The New Meta: JSO-LD, RDF's Microdata, and Schema.org

This chapter is where we start to get a little more technical with our SEO talk. Do not worry, however, because we will be sure to talk through these things in a way that is easy to understand. Even if the title of this chapter looks like a strand of letters that you have never seen put together before, by the end of this chapter you will feel confident in your understanding of each of these things.

In this chapter, we are going to be looking into something called the meta. The meta description, or meta tag, is the small description that Google shows underneath your title and website link in their search results. Meta simply means meta data. Meta data is information about the content of your site. There are different types of tags that you can use on your site for the small description that shows up in Google search results, and we will be looking into each one of these types over the course of this chapter.

First we will continue discussing metatags as a whole. Meta data helps SEO, which is why you should know what it is as well as how you should go about using it. They help SEO by letting Google know what the content of your web page is actually about without Google having to look through your entire site.

First, you will want to figure out if your site is using metatags. To do this, right click on your page and when the menu box pops up, click on "view page source". When you do this, the page will show you the metatags if they are being used. If meta tags show up, definitely take the time to look into them. It is important that you understand the metatags that your own site is using. If your metatags are not relevant to your site or if you are not getting the traffic you would like to see and you want to try something new to increase it, consider changing your metatags.

There are four main types of metatags that people commonly use and that show good success rates in most cases. The first type is called Meta Keywords Attribute. This meta tag is a list of keywords that you want your site to show up in the google search results for. The keywords should also be used in your content of course, but putting them in a metatag can help as well. The second type is called a Title Tag. This metatag shows the title of your site and can help you to show up in the results when someone searches for the title of your page on Google. The next type is called a Meta Description Attribute. This type has a short description of the content of your page within the tag. The last main type is called a Meta Robots Attribute, and this helps those spiders and crawlers know exactly what to do when they get to your site.

Each of these types of metatags have their own time and place to be used. However, some are much more useful than others. For example, Meta Keywords Attribute is not as useful as it used to be. This is because people used to just type in random keywords that they knew would generate a lot of search results even if the words had nothing to do with the content of their site. Google figured this trick out, and now does not put as much weight on Meta Keywords Attribute because they need their search results to always be relevant and helpful to the people who are using their search tool online.

Meta Descriptions Attribute is a lot more helpful. With this tool, Google still puts quite a bit of weight on what you right as your description. This makes this type of meta tag a good tool to use to make your site show up in the searches that you need to be visible in.

Meta Robots Attribute is helpful as well since it tells the spiders and crawlers what to do with your site. This also helps you to show up in the search results that you need and want to be in the most.

Title tags are the most helpful of all of the types of meta tags. These have a high power when looking into the google search results. They're also something that can be seen by people when they are looking at the Google search results. These are actually the things that make the titles of links to sites show up in Google's results list.

Even if you are a beginner, you can use meta tags to better your search engine optimization, or your SEO. You can look up the information or simply eve read through this chapter of our book. It should help you to understand meta tags enough to implement them on your own site. If you are still struggling with meta tags, you can use online tools that are made to help you with them.

Next, we are going to look into some newer ways to better your site that are similar to meta data but that may actually work even better. The first thing we are going to look into is called JSON-LD. JSON-LD is a linked data tool. It allows for people to click on one site and then be brought through multiple other sites. It is easy to implement on your own site and it is easy for your readers to read as well.

The next tool we will look into is called RDFa. RDFa is a tool that stands for resource description framework in attributes. RDFa works with attributes of sites and tells what these attributes are through extensions to more sources of data. This should be capable of providing Google with even more information about your site than typical meta tags can do.

Microdata can be used to describe yourself as well. This is a tool that simply gives names to different pieces of the content on your site to allow it to show up in different Google search result lists. For example, if you write one article about cooking on your blog but you typically write about horses, your cooking article may need to show up in a different google search. This is where microdata can come in handy because it can make that happen for you. This is a tool that is nice for people with multiple businesses or who write a blog about more than one topic.

Schema.org is another tool that can be used. This tool can add a list of different vocabulary words to your site's tags. This can take different pieces of your site, like content, ratings, or your location, and add them all into tags for you website. This can help you to show up in more Google searches while keeping you results in relevant places at all times.

The last tool that we are going to look into is called Facebook Open Graph. This is the tool that allows you to log into many different websites across the internet using your Facebook log in. This is an easy way for people to log into your site and also is an easy way to see and study the types of visitors that are coming to your site. When you know who is visiting your site, you can consider writing specifically for that type of crowd to gain more followers and visitors and increase your SEO. It also allows you to use the Facebook plug ins. These include the like button, comment feature, and the ability for viewers to show your page to their personal Facebook page. This can help spread the word about your website faster than many other methods that we have talked about so far.

Overall, it is clear that there are quite a few tools that can use your SEO. We have covered the best and most helpful tools in this chapter. These tools may seem difficult to use at first, but once you learn how to use them it will become easier and easier. Like anything else, once you practice with these tools you will become better at them and they will provide you with better results. Also, typically tools that require some extra thought and effort are tools that can help you more than things that are easy to use. Everyone would use these if they were easy. Because of this, if you learn how to use even one of these tools you can have the opportunity to really boost your SEO and set yourself apart from your competition.

# Chapter Nine: Where to Start

Now that we have covered these helpful tools, let's spend some time learning how exactly we can start using them. We know that these tools can be a little tricky and somewhat complicated when you first look into them. Because of this, we are going to help you get started. We want you to succeed and we believe that by the end of this chapter, you will be able to start using these tools with ease.

First, let's look into schema.org. Why should you use this tool? As we mentioned before, you should use this tool because it can greatly benefit your SEO. Let's look into what schema.org is in more detail and discuss why exactly it is a tool that you should be using for your site as soon as possible.

First, it is important to know that schema.org is something that people around the world contribute to. It is a joint effort to provide success to every person who knows about and uses the tool. This in itself is a great reason to use schema.org because it is like a community. It is a place where you can support others in their SEO journey and it is a place where they will support you as well.

Another reason to use Schema.org is because it can be used with all of the other tools that we have talked about so far. It is simply a tool that generates vocabulary to provide you with SEO success in the area of microdata. It can be used along with JSON-LD and RDFa, which we talked about in the previous chapter. Both of these tools provide great success and schema.org can make that success even greater.

The first thing that you need to do in order to start using and benefiting from schema.org is familiarize yourself with tags. Luckily, we have already covered this information in the last chapter so you should already be able to check this step off of the list. If you do not yet feel comfortable with tags, consider going back to the information that we covered in the last chapter and reviewing it once again.

Next, you will want to understand what schema markup is. This is simply the rich vocabulary that you use in your site and in your tags. This vocabular is then able to tell google what your content actually means instead of google just seeing the words that you write for everyone to see.

You can then select what type of information you want to mark up on your website and the schema community will help you with the process of finding the right vocabulary to use.

Now let's look into how to get started with JSON-LD. First, let's remind ourselves on why this site is so useful in the first place. JSON-LD makes the data and information on your website show up in a way that is easy for spiders and crawlers to read. This benefits your SEO greatly with just a little bit of effort from your end.

How do we get started with JSON-LD? To start with this tool, you will need four types of keywords. The first type of keyword is the Schema. This keyword is for version control. The next type of keyword is the ID, or identification of the site. The next keyword includes the description and the title. The last keyword includes the type.

You then add properties to each keyword. This helps the spiders and crawlers to know exactly what you mean by each keyword, which helps you to get into the exact Google search results that you want to be in.

You can continue to go deeper into the properties of the keywords including things like product names and even prices. Everything that you add will narrow down your search results to get exactly where you want to be more and more.

Overall, JSON-LD is just a way of controlling how the spiders and crawlers read your site's data. It's a way of controlling how you show up in Google search results. If you are not showing up in the ranking spot you want to be in or if you are showing up in search results that don't fully fit your website's purpose, JSON-LD is a great place to start the process of getting your site to where you ultimately want it to be. With the details we just covered, you should be able to use this tool pretty easily as well.

Next, let's look into Facebook Open Graph. Before we look into how you can use Facebook Open Graph, let's look into why exactly you should be using it. This tool is good to use because it simply provides you with so much information. It tells you what types of users are visiting your site and what content they enjoy the most. It also helps greatly to spread the word of your site. It allows your site visitors to share your content on their personal Facebook pages, which in turns makes sure that your content is seen by many more people. It shows on Facebook how many likes and shares your content receives, so people may be more willing to click on it when they see that it has been interacted with by many other people. It also allows for comments. You can use these comments as reviews. If you have some extra time you could even respond to these comments to help grow your SEO and site visitor appreciation at the same time.

You can add Facebook Open Graph to your website through the use of tags. The tags should show what the content of your website is about so that it can be found by people who are either looking for that type of content or at least people who are already interested in that type of content. This also again helps Google to know what your site is about so that it can sort it into the right search engine results.

After adding the tags you want, you will have to change the html code of your website. When you change this code to include Facebook, the open graph program will be added to your site. You can then add a like button to your page with an iFrame or with a Java Script SDK placed in your tags.

You will then need to add Open Graph meta tags. The meta tags that are required are og:title, og:type,og:Image, and og:URL. If you want to, you can also add the optional codes which are og:description, og:site_name and og:app_id. Of course, the more tags you add the better off your results will be, so it is a good idea to add these extra and optional tags if you have the time and ability to do so.

Once you have completed all of these steps, your site should be all set to work with Facebook Open Graphs. Just these few simple steps will bring you large amounts of information that you can use to optimize your site, and it will also bring your site way more exposure than it would get without the use of Open Graphs.

Schema.org, JSON-LD, and Facebook Open Graph are all great tools to use on your site. Now that we have covered how to get started in each of these areas, you should be able to implement these tools into your own site. They may seem complicated at first, but with the information you have learned in this book and a little bit of practice, we know that you have the ability to succeed with these great SEO tools.

# Chapter Ten: Final Powerful SEO Tools

We have covered a lot of information in this book so far. We started by talking about what SEO means, and now you just finished learning some of its most complicated pieces. In this final chapter, we want to share with you some final tools that will help you greatly to have the best SEO that you can possibly get.

First we will look into research tools for SEO. We looked a little bit into keyword research earlier in the book but just to refresh your memory, keyword research helps you to come up with keywords and it also helps you to understand the power behind each different keyword. They help you to see how keywords are performing on the internet today before you decide to use them on your own site.

Wordstream has a free keyword research tool. This tool lets you pick a niche and gives you lists of suggestions to use for the actual keyword within that niche. It can be used for thirty free searches and you get a seven day free trial after your thirty free searches are used up, so you can actually use this helpful site at no cost for quite a long time.

Soolve is tool that is always free. It shows you the keywords that are typed in most often on a variety of different search engines when you give it a topic that you are interested in. It is a great tool for coming up with keywords that you may not have been able to think up on your own.

Ubersuggest is an extremely fast and easy to use tool. It is also free. When you give it a topic, it instantly gives you a huge list of keywords that you can look through and choose from. It is a great tool to use if you want something that is easy, free, and something that does not take much time from your already busy schedule.

Ahrefs Keyword Explorer is a great tool for a more advanced version of keyword research. It has a huge number of keywords in its system and it adds new words to its database every single month. This means you can keep getting new results from this tool if you need to use it on the same topics more than once. The topics it has now are probably enough, though, since it has close to one million keywords in its database. It looks into clicks, clicks per search, and return rate when deciphering which keywords are the best. It works with three types of keyword ideas including autocomplete, questions, and suggestions.

SEMrush Keyword Magic Tool can be helpful as well. It has less keywords in its database, but still plenty to help you find what you need. It shows you a graph of how much the keywords have been used over the course of the last year. If you are a person who learns well from visuals, this is a good tool for you to choose.

Google AdWords Keyword Planner is of course a good research tool for keywords as well. It is a part of Google so it helps a lot with your SEO in Google's search results specifically. This tool is great to use because it's just easy. It is simple to use and provides great results.

Next, let's look into optimization tools. Optimization tools are of course important because the whole point of SEO is to optimize our search engine results. It's even in the name of the thing we are looking into (SEO). These are tools that help to make sure you show up high in the rankings of the Google search results.

One of the best optimization tools is a tool that we have already talked about in this book called Google Analytics. As we talked about earlier, Google Analytics shows how your site is performing online. It shows who is visiting your site, how long they are staying, what they are clicking on, and what else they are interacting with. It can tell you the peak times for visitors on your site and the type of people who are following you in categories based on things like gender and age. This information can help you to see how your SEO is doing and it can also help you to get to know your audience. If you know your audience, you can cater to them and make the number of viewers you have continue to grow.

Google Page Speed Insights is a good optimization tool as well. This tool checks both your site speed and the usability of your site. As we learned earlier, both of these things are very important factors when trying to better your SEO. This tool even gives you ideas on how you could possibly improve your site speed and the usability of your web page. It tells you what to change as well as what to keep the same with its user experience scores.

Moz Local Listing Score is a great tool to use when you are looking into your local SEO. This tool allows you to see where you stand compared to other local sites in terms of SEO. Based on the information you find with this tool, you should be able to optimize your SEO even more. You can continue doing what you are doing if you are at the top. If there is competition that is ranking above you, consider looking into their SEO tactics to see what is working so well for them. You can change your game plan to match or outscore theirs after gathering this information.

Even just simply using the incognito window on your computer's web browser can be a great optimization tool. When you use the incognito window, you can see where your site actually stands in the Google search. You cannot do this with a typical browser window because Google knows that you own your own site, so they will make it show up high in the results for you. This does not mean that it shows up in the same place for everyone else. When you use the incognito window, you see what everyone else in the world sees when they find your web page. Based on your findings with this tool, you can look back into your tactics on your you can better optimize your search engine result rankings.

Next, let's look into tools that can help you with link building. We know that link building is extremely important and that it can allow you to build your SEO faster and easier than any other tactic that you can ever do. We also know, however, that it is a challenging thing to do. Because of this, these link building tools can be extremely helpful.

The first tool we will look into is the social media site Instagram. Instagram is actually a great tool to use to find links. This is because many businesses and blogs promote their sites on Instagram. This is also because the site owners typically take a very personal presence on this site and they tend to be very friendly with their followers. To try to get links with this tool, you will want to follow people that have similar businesses or similar blogs to you. You could also follow small business owners that live in the same town as you are that live in a town nearby. When you follow these people, they will probably follow you back. You will then want to begin an online relationship with them by commenting on and liking their posts. Once you feel you have built a strong online relationship with them, you can ask them to link to your site within their content sometime. This is not a tool that is guaranteed to work, but it does work often so it is definitely worth a try. Plus, you'll be adding exposure and content for your site while you work on the relationship so even if they say no, your work will not be a wasted effort.

Another great link building tool is Moz Link Explorer. This is a free tool that allows you to see where on the internet your site and your content is linked to from. When you can see where on the internet people are able to click and be redirected to your site, you are able to judge how you are doing in the link building department. If you have a large amount of links coming to you, you are probably doing pretty well. If you have no links, then link building is definitely something that you will want to start spending more time on when you work on your site.

Ahref's Backlink Checker is a great tool as well. We looked into another one of Ahref's tools earlier on in this chapter, and this tool is just as high quality as the last one that we looked into. This tool allows you to pick any website, copy and paste their URL into the search bar, and figure out where they are linked to from everywhere on the internet. This can be a great tool to use if you are wanting to know how your competitors are getting their link building from. You can copy and paste the URL of your competition's website into the search bar and see where their links are coming from. You can then use this list of links as a list of ideas on who you can contact in your link building journey. You can try contacting the same people that your competitor did, or you can try contacting similar pages and people. You know that your competitors link building is working, however, so you will definitely want to do something like what they are doing since they are finding the success that you are searching so hard for.

Another really helpful tool in look building is a site called Guest Post Tracker. This site keeps a running log of websites across the internet that are currently accepting submissions for guest bloggers. If you use this site, it takes away some of the time that you would have had to spend researching which blogs you should reach out to. It also gives you the peace of mind that at least when you reach out to these people, you already know that guest blogging is something that they at the very least consider. You are not going to annoy them or offend them by asking to a be a guest blogger on their site, because they say that they are actively searching for and accepting guest bloggers. This site does cost money to use, but it is just a onetime fee of 99 dollars.

Lastly, let's look into tools that can help you with your web analytics. As we learned earlier in this book, these tools help you to understand who is viewing your page, when they are viewing your page, and what they are doing once they get to your page. These tools can be helpful because they help you to get to know your audience so that you are able to consider catering specifically to them. Typically when you know your audience, you are able to help grow your site viewers quickly.

The first tool that is extremely helpful with web analytics is Google Analytics. We already mentioned this tool so we won't look into it in detail again. We will just mention that this tool works well because it is run by Google and Google also runs the search results that you are working so hard to stand out in.

Another great web analytics tool is Woopra. Woopra is a tool that shows the tracking of real time analytics. This tool is unique because it not only lets you track your site visitors, but it lets you interact with them as well. If you are looking to get to know your site visitors on a more personal level or if you have a lot of time to be online while people are checking out your site, then this tool is definitely for you. Woopra has different plans ranging from free to a few different price points. The higher priced options of course come with more capabilities than the free and lower priced options.

Clicky is another helpful tool when it comes to web analytics. It does the typical web analytics tracking of people that visit your site, but it comes with another feature as well. Clicky allows you to view the actions that people are doing live while they are visiting your site. For example, you could choose a viewer and watch what they are seeing on the website. You can pay attention to what they click on and how much time they spend on each page. You can actually experience this type of tracking instead of reading it through data. This is an interesting twist and can make web analytics a little more fun. This site is also free to use, which is a huge added bonus.

Kissmetrics is another great web analytics tool. This tool again watches the visitors that come to your site and analyzes their actions. The cool thing about this site, however, is that it stores the data that it finds, It then takes this data and analyzes it, looking for patterns and behavioral changes that happen over time. This can help you to be even more aware of what is happening with the visitors of your site.

Overall, it is clear that there are many sites we can use to better our SEO. We only mentioned a few of the best tools in this book, while in reality there are hundreds of tools available online that are made to help you maximize your SEO. There are more research tools to help you get the best keywords. More optimization tools to ensure your website is in tip-top shape, more link building tools to make a difficult process a little bit easier, and more web analytic tools so that you can understand your site visitors even better. If you use any tools at all, they will help you to improve your SEO. You can use one tool from each of these sections or you can use multiple tools to receive advice and help from multiple different sources and varying points of view. You can stick with the first site you try or you can try every one of these tools until you find one that you love using. You can even read through this list and decide that you do not care for any of these powerful tools and that you would rather find your own different tool to find online. We know that you now have enough knowledge on SEO to make educated and informed decisions on what is best for you and for your own site. We hope this chapter gave you a good idea of where to start with powerful SEO tools and that you are able to use these sites to benefit your SEO and your business and website overall.

# Conclusion

We have covered a lot of information together in this book. When we started out, we were discussing the most basic topics from what SEO stands for to how Google works. We then moved on to talking about Google ranking factors and how to rank well in the search engine results.

We looked into keyword research and we learned that this is the most important step of search engine optimization. We talked about finding keywords, how to tell if a keyword will bring you success in SEO, as well as how to use keywords and where to place them in your content.

We then talked about all of the different things that you need to be aware of when you are working on bettering your SEO. We mentioned things like on page SEO, structure, site load speed, duplicate content, usability, readability, and mobile support. We talked about how to accelerate traffic to your site and how to be featured in Google's featured snippets in order to receive more traffic to your site.

We discussed link building in detail and talked about how this is the most powerful tool that we have in SEO. We learned how to get others to link to our site as well as what to do and what not to do when it comes to building links.

We covered social media sites like Facebook, Twitter, Instagram, Pinterest, and LinkedIn. We talked about why these sites are important for SEO and how exactly you can use them to benefit your overall SEO.

We looked into web analytics and what it can do for us. We learned why this tool is important and how we can use it. We talked about terms like acquisition, organic search reports, segmentation, and more. We learned that this told helps us to measure the success of our site and shows us how we can improve as well.

We learned about problems that may arise while we work with our SEO like not showing up in google searches or dropping our rankings significantly. We learned what causes these problems as well as how we can fix them when they do happen to occur.

We talked about local SEO, how it is different from normal SEO, and why it is important for your business. We learned how local SEO is ranked in google search results as well as how to improve these rankings through things like citations and reviews. We talked about the difference that can be made through something as simple as phots or videos.

We learned a few of the more complicated SEO procedures including JSON-LD, RDFa, Microdata, and Schema.org. We talked about how to get started using each of these told and learned the benefits that each one carries.

We ended by covering many more tools that you can use in your SEO journey including research tools, optimization tools, link building tools, and web analytics tools.

You may have been a beginner to SEO when you started this book, but by now we know that you are ready to succeed in this area. You have all of the knowledge you need and every tool you'll want to have a great SEO for your website. We wish you luck on your SEO journey and we are glad that we were able to help you get to this point.

Printed in Great Britain
by Amazon